patchwork
A POET'S GUIDE TO LOVE
catarine hancock

central
avenue

This book is a work of creative expression. Although it draws upon the author's personal experiences, it includes fictionalized elements, alterations, and composite characters for literary effect. As such, it should not be read as a literal or factual account. Any resemblance to actual persons, living or dead, or to actual events is purely coincidental or used in a fictionalized manner.

Published by Central Avenue Poetry,
an imprint of Central Avenue Marketing Ltd.
centralavenuepublishing.com

PATCHWORK: A POET'S GUIDE TO LOVE

Trade Paperback: 978-1-77168-412-5
Ebook: 978-1-77168-413-2

Printed in United States of America

1. POETRY / Love 2. POETRY / Women Authors

1 3 5 7 9 10 8 6 4 2

for all the lovers
who never fail
to stitch themselves
back together

from the poet:

and love, to me, is this inescapable, destined ruination. it is the culmination of everything i've ever yearned for and everything i've ever feared. it is the bullet and the bandage. it is the beginning and the end. i would have died for it when i was younger. and now that i'm older, i think i always have been. with every hello and every goodbye. with every piece gained and every piece lost. bit by bit. and i let it.

oh god, i can't help but let it.

love is a needle and thread
and i am the tapestry
it blends itself into me
it expands me
creating something better
every time i have outgrown it
every rip in the seams
carefully mended

love has made me into patchwork
i am sewn together
by a rainbow of threads
some thick
some thin
some strong
some frail

every stitch
a memory
of somebody
i once
knew

every knot
an echo
of somebody
i once
was

some of you will read this book and you will think i am beating the same dead horse, that i am digging up the same grave—the one i swore to have buried and walked away from all those years ago.

but this is not about just one person. it is about all of them. it is about all of them who whittled me down, who contorted me into something small or broken or angry. it is about the one who lied to me for months. it is about the one who gave me panic attacks because his version of events was so different from mine that i did not trust my reality. it is about the one who asked me to stick around until he figured out if he'd rather be with me or the girl he cheated on me with. it is about the one who tried to fuck my friend three days after we broke up and attempted to blame me for it. it is about all of them. each one who carved a mark into me.

so yes, i have buried them all. i have walked away from their tombstones and i have not looked back. this is not a rehashing.

but i have the marks still.

and some things, you cannot bury and leave behind.

i.

first love is
the threading
of the needle

the beginning
of what will hopefully
be something
beautiful

you don't know exactly
what it is you're doing yet
but you're ready to
create that first stitch

i yearned for love when i was younger—
i was a romantic from the moment
i learned to read.

hopeless doesn't even begin
to describe it.

i counted down the days
to the start of my first love.
i'd wonder what they'd look like,
imagine the cadence of their voice,
the feel of their hands.

i had many things to keep myself busy
in the meantime, of course,
but i was the first to raise my hand
as volunteer when love finally asked,
"who's next?"

"me! oh, me!" i cried,
and oh, was i happy
when love picked

me.

finally. the hopeless romantic gets her romance.

if only she'd remembered the hopeless part.

there was something so *meant-to-be* about it. of course he was a writer just like me. of course he was a romantic at heart. of course he was misunderstood by everyone else. of course i was the only one who really got him.

it was all lining up to be so, so perfect. i couldn't believe i'd been so lucky. i was completely convinced i'd gotten it right on the very first try.

you're so beautiful
he'd tell me,

and it wasn't the first time
i'd heard it

but it was the first time
it felt like it really counted

for our fleeting, precious moment,
the world seemed
to shine and shimmer
like never before.

has it always been this beautiful?
i wondered.

or is it him?

is our love the sunlight
through the trees
and the sweetness in the air?

and i believed it was.

of course i did.

wouldn't you?

he was the
center
of my universe.

my sun;
the golden star
i orbited my days
around.

i was so happy to
spin and spin and spin
for him.

i would have basked
in his light forever
if i could have.

this is what it's like to fall in love when you're young:

you give them everything, because how could you not? being young and in love is an intoxicating feeling. it's an addiction. the butterflies, the sparks, the adrenaline rush—you become hooked on all of it. you'd do almost anything to feel that way, anything to hold on to it for as long as possible. so when i talk about the people i loved when i was young—when i was thirteen, when i was sixteen–and i say, *i gave them everything*, i mean it. because that's what you do when you're young and love comes knocking at your door. you give it everything. you just don't know any better.

i'd like to relive them, i think. the memories of us. not for him, but for the feeling: the heady rush of first love. that feeling that everything had fallen into place because i had somebody. i still feel that, but it's not so invincible anymore. it worries, now. it wavers.

so i'd like to experience that again: when love wasn't terrifying in the slightest. not a day goes by when it's not scary now.

it was so beautiful
when it was just
us

take me back
to the time
when love was
just two people

no outside factors
no reality checks

take me back
to the time
when love was
blissfully
simple

my mother used to tell me i loved being in love. she'd say it with a shake of her head, admonishment coating each word.

i didn't understand why it was a bad thing, to love love. to chase that bubbling, fluttering joy. it was beautiful, was it not?

even after the end, even after i could hardly eat or breathe or speak, i chased that high. i flung myself into the abyss over and over again because i loved that exhilarating fall.

now i know what a horrid curse it is to love being in love, to throw yourself knowingly to your doom because you love the wind on your face.

i know, and yet—

i still jump.

every time.

first love is thrilling, isn't it? at least, it is while you're in it. not so much when it ends.

i must admit, i remember very little about my first love. oh, i remember his name. i'd know him in an instant if i saw him in a crowd, to be sure. but so much of us has faded. i could not tell you what his voice sounds like anymore; i could not begin to describe the song that was his laugh.

i'll tell you what i do remember, though, in painstaking, explicit detail: the night that it ended. when he ripped my heart into shreds with his bare hands. when love showed me just how cruel it could be. that was an agony i felt in my very soul. the scars of it are etched there even now. and perhaps part of me, despite my blissful, lovesick ignorance, knew that was how it would end.

but that is the beauty of it. even when you know, you reach for it anyway.

nothing is as beautiful
as falling in love
for the first time

each butterfly something
you've never felt before

each blossom something
that will never bloom
the same way
again

nothing is as horrible
as getting your heart broken
for the first time

each ache something
you've never felt before

each break something
that will never be
completely mended
again

ii.

if first love
becomes the first stitch
first heartbreak
is the first tear

the first snapping of the thread
the first fraying of the fabric

the moment you realize
this won't be easy

love wrapped me in honey glaze
and rose gold hues,
cocooned me in flowered cotton
and the bliss of youth.

life was limitless—
life was *new*;
so much left to learn.
too much left to lose.

and i didn't know it,
eyes closed to the truth,
so i didn't see it coming:
the pain of losing

you.

the way your first love ends
will always stay with you.

he picked another girl over me:
i am forever afraid of being left
for somebody better.

he told me she was just a friend:
those words will never fail
to make my stomach turn.

he came back when she rejected him:
i am the second choice,
the backup.

there's always somebody
they'd prefer to be with
if they could.

and it doesn't matter
how many times it's proven
to be untrue.

there are some things
that are simply so ingrained in me,
threaded through every part of me,
that no matter how hard i work,
no matter how much time has passed,
there will always be pieces
of that pain
left.

it's so funny, in hindsight, how naive i was. that night, when he told me he had feelings for her, i was stunned. *how could that be possible?* i had thought. *he's with me.* but now, i look back on it, and all the signs were there from the beginning. he loved me, sure, but i was always, in some ways, the second choice. he would've had her if he'd gotten the chance. he'd even told me as much: *well, i don't see her that much, but i see you all the time.* that's what he said. i would've run in the other direction if somebody said those words to me today. but young, lovesick me? she bought it, hook, line, and sinker. that was good enough for her. she didn't know any better.

i don't hold any anger for him anymore—i haven't in nearly ten years. he was just a boy, after all, figuring it all out just like i was. i would like to be able to say i would've done the same if i'd been in his shoes. but i know i wouldn't have.

i've always loved in tunnel vision.

this can't be happening,
i thought to myself
not to me
not to us

but it was
it was

you will always wonder if you did something to deserve it when this happens. and i know i didn't: i had been kind and patient and loving. i had been myself, which he had always said was a good thing. but i still wondered if maybe i did. if maybe the reasons he fell in love with me were also what made him walk away.

it was only a small piece—
what he took.
only a small piece,
and yet it felt as though
half of my soul had been
ripped out of me.

it was just puppy love,
the adults said.
nothing like the real thing.

but i had never experienced
the real thing.
how was i supposed to know
the difference?

and god,
if what they say is true,
if *real love* is
more
consuming,
more
devastating,
more
beautiful,
more
terrifying,

then how on earth
am i supposed
to survive that
when *puppy love*
nearly killed me?

if i sort through
my memories
i can hardly remember
anything from this time

i just remember the darkness
that seemed to swirl around me
the anger i wrapped myself in

the betrayal and the pain
following me wherever i went

he came back, of course.
they always do.

despite the heartbroken fog
i spent my days shrouded in,
i knew it was only
a matter
of time.

it didn't take much convincing
for me to let him in again

i had missed the golden world
we'd lived in
i wanted it back

i wanted *him* back

i opened my heart
to him again
and he gave back
the piece of it he'd stolen

i expected it to pop
right back into place
for me to be good as new again

but the piece was chipped
and cracked
all bent out of shape
from when he'd wrenched it
out of me
blackened and rotted from
the pain he'd caused

irreparably broken

there was no going back.
there was no way to return
to the sweetness of before.

gone was the glimmering sheen
of first love and innocence.

now i was paranoid.
now i was worried.

and yes,
there was still love.
lots of it.

but now
it was tainted.

and we both had to
live with that.

so,
when the end raised
its ugly, snarling head,
i did not run.

i did not beg,
however badly
i wanted to.

i knew.
i had always
known.

i let it come,
and i did not
linger to watch
it go.

i was not surprised when it ended again. i think i knew, deep down, that this second chance i'd given him wasn't going to last, that he'd squander it in some foolish way. just a boy, remember?

i think i spent most of those four months before the end grieving him, grieving us, because i knew it was only a matter of time.

and in a way, i was grieving me, too.

because the young, innocent girl i'd been?

she was never coming back.

some part of me
burnt into nothing that night
and from the ashes
rose somebody strong enough
to walk away
and never look back

i hope you're happy. genuinely, i do. i hope you grew into somebody kind. i hope you never lost your vulnerability. i hope you never stopped writing. i hope you learned from me.

i hope you remember me, but i hope i don't haunt you.

you are
woven through me
even now

i never once asked myself why i loved him.

i loved him because of course i did. him, with the lopsided smile and the calloused hands and the ink-stained fingertips. him, with the sugar-sweet promises and the hallowed secrets and the bleeding heart. he gave me love.

he gave me poetry.

and that was everything in the end, was it not?

i often wonder what it would be like to run into him. to see him in the aisle of a bookstore or in line at a coffee shop on one of my visits home. i wonder how he has aged, if he still looks mostly the same or if life has hardened or softened him in some way. i wonder if his hands are still calloused the way they were when we were young. i wonder if his eyes will still have that same warmth. i wonder if being in the same room with him again would make it feel like a graveyard, if the dead love between us would shiver and quake. i wonder if any of that decade-old anger i haven't felt in years would rear its ugly head. i wonder if we'd even know how to talk to each other. i wonder if i'd recognize him at first glance.

i wonder, more than anything, if he'd recognize me.

you weren't the one for me
in any lifetime

but i think in every lifetime
you were always going to be
the first

iii.

eventually
you pick the needle back up
and thread it once more

every rip must be mended
at some point after all
and you are trying
to create something
long-lasting

not one to be discouraged
after one failed stitch

i searched for signs of my first love in everyone. i think, even now, more than a decade later, i still do. but i especially did it in those first few months, after he was gone and out of my life for good. i scoured people for traces of his smile, for the cadence of his voice, for the melody of his laugh. it wasn't that i missed him—though i'm sure i did—it was that he was what love looked like. for all i knew, he was what love would always be.

i expected the next love
to feel like him.

i didn't yet understand
that no love was ever the same.

nothing would ever feel like him
again.

in some ways,
he was in every love
that came after him.

he was in their dimples,
their mouths, their hands.

he was in their laughs
and their smiles,
and he was, of course,
in their wreckage, too.

he was always there
standing beside them
among the ruins.

but my first love was also
in me.

woven into my hopes and my poems,
wedged down in between my teeth.

built into the very foundation
of the way i loved

and the way i left.

by god,
was he in the way
i left.

it took longer to heal than i wanted to admit at the time. that's usually how it goes. i wanted to be over it. past it. i desperately needed it to be in the rearview mirror. so i tried, so very hard, to find a new love with another person. i didn't grasp that i didn't need to move on to another person to move on from him.

i tried to plant new seeds with other people.

overwatered every single one.

eventually, love bloomed again. it was a different shape: harder in some spots, softer in others, sharpened corners where there hadn't been any before. but it was still love.

even now, i am still awed by love's transformation every time it reappears in my life. how it is always new but somehow still the same.

learning to trust again
was the hardest part

i could not fall blindly
anymore

only taking steps
towards the edge
after asking
a dozen questions

only deciding to jump
after cushioning my fall
with a thousand reassurances

i tried to close myself off

tried to get really good
at keeping people

out

and keeping my feelings

in

tried more than anything
to keep myself
safe

but i just couldn't
stop

the truth is
i just think life is
a little less bright
if you wrap your heart
in barbed wire
and snarl at anybody
who tries to show
you kindness

i'm incapable of walling my heart off. i could never do that to myself. i could never do it to other people, either. i know that i am filled with love and it is worth experiencing. i will not deprive people of it. not my friends, not my lovers, not the stray cats on the street, not the random person who holds the door for me. i wear my heart on my sleeve and i am tired of pretending that it's my greatest weakness. it's not. it never has been.

but even knowing
you are filled with love
does not make
falling for somebody new
any less terrifying

when you have
so much to give
you want it to be
worth something

and nothing is worse
than somebody treating
your love like
it's worthless

you know those marble statues where the fabric is carved so beautifully it looks like real cloth? like if you reached out, your fingers would brush against silk and not stone. that's how the promises i made to myself—the promises they would each make to me—felt every time i crashed to the ground.

i thought i'd land on downy pillows and plush blankets. we'd made it look so soft and gentle. but it was still slamming into solid rock each time.

the ending was always the same.

— *illusion*

and yet / despite the ruin it may cause / despite the scars it may leave behind / you cannot help but take that chance / each time hoping it may be different / each time wishing the ending might change / because one day / it will / one day the glass won't shatter / one day the foundation won't sink / one day it won't be a crash landing / one day / they will stay / and so will you / and isn't that chance / however small and coveted it may be / isn't that worth leaping for?

iv.

but try as you might
the stitches won't hold

some are too tight
some are too loose

the needle shakes
in your hand

are you doing something wrong?

this is not coming together
the way you thought it would

the wrong love eventually starts feeling
like wearing shoes that are half a size too small:

you can ignore the tightness for a while,
because it fits well enough.

but eventually,
the discomfort catches up to you,
and even the smallest of steps
become painful.

i realized we weren't meant to be
two years before we went our separate ways.

but that's how long
i tried to change the ending.

i poured love into us,
tried to tip the scales in our favor,
said
look at all these wonderful things about us.
look at how we laugh at the same jokes
and know how to touch one another
and want the best for each other.

and fate shook her head.
took my hand in hers,
said
but look at how you are straining in your own skin,
look at how you bite your tongue every day,
look at the distance already there.
look at how it grows.

but we love each other,
i said.

fate sighed,
my dear, no amount of love
can make two mismatched pieces fit together.
not unless you mutilate them into something
they never were.

i tell you
i make everything
into poetry
in my head

my life—
it is all poetry
to me
it always has been

every experience
written in ink
in my mind

and you
of course
are poetry
too

i make
metaphors
out of your mouth
similes
out of your sweetness

and when it is over
i will make poetry
out of that too
the way i always do

i'll find beauty
in the way i go
the pieces i'll leave behind

the pieces of you
i'll take
and i'll immortalize
the gentleness
with which you loved me

look how beautiful it was
i'll say
and look how beautiful
i can still make it out
to be

in another life,
maybe i marry you.

i fold the laundry
and we cook dinner together
and hold each other tight
through the night
because in that life,
i figured out
how to sleep next to you
(i never really could in this one).

in another life,
maybe the person
i'm meant to be with
is you,
and i do not feel suffocated
by the thought
of putting a ring
on my finger.

in another life,
maybe it is enough for me,
what you gave me,
which was, in most ways,
never lacking, or wrong.

in another life,
maybe i simply am
different,
but in all honesty,
i cannot imagine a life
where i am content to

spend my years feeling
so small.

i loved you more than anything else in the world once,

and that was still not enough to keep you.

one day, i woke up and realized
that it was all pointless.

the begging and the crying
and the contorting and the
hypothesizing and the wondering
was all being done for nothing.
there was no good ending.

god,
we were destroying each other.

why must i always be the one
who sees it first?

fine, i'll say it:

i'm glad it didn't work.

i will always be grateful
that i got to love you,
but i am so glad

it didn't work.

it would've been nice, you know?

to have been able
to keep you forever

you cannot get caught up in the what ifs. easier said than done, i know. i spent years trapped in their jaws. but you cannot let them hold you prisoner. there is no point in ruminating on what could have been. what if they had been different, what if you had been different, what if this, what if that—it builds a cage around you, eventually.

there is no what if, my dear.

there is only what is.

we tried so hard
to buff out the blemishes,
put so much time into
ironing out the wrinkles,

but the shine always wore off.
the creases always reappeared.

eventually
it became work—
monotonous,
tiresome
work.

love is not monotonous—
it becomes simple,
reliable.

it's not monotonous
to become something
you can count on.

love is not tiresome—
it becomes challenging,
rewarding.

it's not tiresome
to become something
that makes you grow.

know the difference.

to put it plainly:

love is *never* boring when you are with the right person.

the steady routine is something you cherish. the small moments are some of your biggest joys.

that's not to say it's always exciting. it's not.

but when you're with the right person, you can be bored together. they're your partner. your best friend. and when you're bored with somebody like that?

well, then life—and love—is never boring.

eventually
you'll move on
and i will be glad
for your happiness

but i will always
always
wonder what life
would have been like
if we had been made
for each other
the way we once
believed we were

i watch you love her and it's easy
like a reflex
like it never was with me

how tiring it must have been
loving me but always feeling
like you had
to work for it

it's strange to be the last girlfriend before the one.
the one they say forever to
and it's not a lie,
the one who fits into their life
the way i never did.

it's strange because i don't want to marry you.
i don't wish it was me.
i don't even think of you much at all anymore,
and my life is better now without you in it, but—

it's still weird, isn't it?
to know that it was so close.
to know that if the timeline was shifted,
if i were the one who came along
just a couple years later,
after all the growing and the maturing
i had begged for had happened,
it might have been me.

but it's not me, and i'm glad it's not,
but i'm also glad that it's somebody.

at least somebody out there
gets the version of you
i deserved
but never got.

you know, one time we kissed and i swear to god our wedding flashed before my very eyes. and when we pulled apart, i knew you'd felt it too—you even said, "wow, that felt like how i'd kiss you on our wedding day." i so rarely think of you now, just in small flashes or bittersweet moments, but i remember that kiss, down to the flutter of your eyelashes.

it's been years since we last spoke, years since you cursed me for the wreckage i left in my wake. sometimes it hardly feels like i ever knew you at all, the person i was when i was with you even less so. half the time i remember us and i think—fondly, to be fair—what the fuck was i even doing with you? but i did love to romanticize our mismatch.

so anyway, i don't even really remember how it felt to love you and you'll probably marry her and there's a lot you did that i haven't quite forgiven you for but one time, you kissed me and it felt like the rest of my life. and i think, maybe that's the blanket i'll wrap you in as i tuck you away into the back of my mind. forget all the anger and disconnect and the way we crumbled. there was at least one moment where you and i made sense.

v.

you think you're getting
the hang of it
despite the lumps
and jagged corners

it's your story
and despite its flaws
you find it beautiful

then one day
someone new arrives
and asks you for the needle

let me show you how it's done
they say

and though you've never trusted
somebody else with it before
you decide to trust them

but when you hand over
the needle and thread
they do not create
something beautiful

instead they set them aside
and with their bare hands
they take the tapestry
and shred it

there will always be the *one*.

the one who weasels their way
into the very heart of you,
who offers promises dipped
in nectar, sweet and ripe
and yours for the taking.

and you won't understand why
they've chosen you,
how you've won them,
but then it will be over.

and you will understand then.
you will understand very well.

the girl i was sits
in a crystal cocoon,
the surface glistening,
and the edges smooth.

on her face sits a blissful smile,
and her heart is unmarred,
she carries no bruises;
she is yet to be scarred.

i wish i could get to her
but the crystal won't break;
i just want to reach her,
to tell her to *wait.*

don't believe him, i'd say,
don't fall for his lies!
don't let him have you,
no matter how much he tries.

but the girl i was sits
in a crystal cocoon,
completely unaware
of the damage he'll do.

and i can only watch.

when it's done,
and all that's left
is the rubble to pick through
and the dead things to bury,
you will ask yourself why.

you will dig through heaps
of twisted metal and broken glass
and question what made you do it
in the first place.

how did you not see
the destruction lurking
just around the corner?
how could you not smell
the storm in the air?

you will hate yourself,
because we all do at first.
after all, it is much easier
than trying to hate them.

i can't even remember how i used to love
before you bent me out of shape

was it something kind?
something soft?

did i once love
without so much teeth and claw?

i built a dream world around him
a house with white shutters
a full bookshelf
and a warm fire
a kitchen filled with fresh vegetables
and a piano in the den

a picture-perfect dreamscape

and then
of course
i woke up
to a home with creaking floorboards
and peeling paint
doors hanging from rusting hinges

and he
was simply nowhere
to be found

let's pretend to fall in love.
will that make it easier
to keep you around?

you'll kiss me hard enough
that i won't notice how your eyes
are open.

you'll run your hands up my thighs
to shut down any conversation
that may be a little too close for comfort.

i'll tell you everything you never asked to hear
and act like i don't know you aren't listening.

but it could be fun,
pretending to be in love.

pretending we are more than hungry
mouths and bored hands.

pretending i don't crave you endlessly
while you are ever so slowly
getting bored
of me.

all loves stay with you forever,
and most of the time
i am grateful for that.

but him—
him, i wish
i could lock in the past
and he would stay there.

i won't waste time
going over all of it again
but just know that i remember
all of it
even now.

unfortunately
i will always
remember.

i used to say
i let him make a shell out of me
slowly drain me until i was empty
until i was nothing but a husk
of a person

but you can't *let* somebody
do something
if you don't know
they're doing it

i didn't know
until it was too late
until i was so deep in it
that i couldn't even
tell it wasn't normal

so i didn't *let* him
do anything to me

he simply did it so slowly
i didn't notice
until i was already
withered

until i was already
broken

that was the worst part, honestly: how i changed.
how that so-called love rotted me from the inside out.
i became a paranoid, twisted, wretched thing,
a starved dog who bit at every hand who tried to feed her
because it wasn't his, though he wasn't doing
much to feed me either.

and everyone could see it.

everyone but me.

i would have loved you if you'd let me—
but the truth is that i loved you anyway.

i loved you enough to rip myself to shreds over it.

i etched your indifference into my skin,
your boredom the knife.
whittled myself into something i thought
you would like, would appreciate, would desire—

i twisted myself into knots
to be easy.

i tossed my standards and expectations
into a grave and left them to rot.

and in the end, did it matter?
did you stay?

did you take my bloodied hands
and say, *enough*?

i would have loved you if you'd let me,
i had said as you'd left,
spitting the words like some sorceress's
curse.

but when i looked in the mirror
and saw my reflection—
all my missing parts,
all my scarred and ragged flesh,

and my heart, remolded into

the shape of your mouth,
beating your name in some
off-kilter, broken rhythm—

oh, yes,
there is no doubt:
i loved you
anyway.

and when time keeps moving
and i love you still

what then?

what then, what then, what then?

were you some karmic justice
sent from the universe?
an act of divine punishment
ordered by some higher power
for a crime i committed in a past life?

because i really don't know
what i did
to deserve you,
and i mean that
in the worst possible sense.

my best skill
has always been
finding the silver lining

so of course
in the aftermath of him
i tried to unearth
something like
a bright side

i tried to look
at the glass
as half-full

i learned something
didn't i?
isn't that something
to be grateful for?

but even my cock-eyed
optimism couldn't
save me

i didn't deserve it.
the words were sewn
into the sinew of me.
my bones creaked
under the weight of them.

i just didn't
deserve it.

it wasn't your fault. you know that, right? it's not your fault that you trusted them and they betrayed you. you weren't too much or too little. this wasn't your fault. they should've known better than to treat you that way. place the blame on them, not on you.

and after the storm has cleared
and all that lies around you
is wreckage,
there is but one thing to do:

rebuild
and start again.

vi.

for a while
you can do nothing
but sit amongst
the tattered remnants
clutch the shreds
helplessly in your hands

but eventually
you pick up
the needle and thread
guide it through
the rips and tears
bringing the pieces
together again

recreating what
they destroyed
crafting it into
something even more
beautiful
than before

when it was over, i sat back and thought,

that's it?
that's all?

and through my heartbroken daze,
a small kernel of hope whispered to me,
see? perhaps it didn't matter so much
after all.

I WAS ALWAYS MEANT FOR MORE THAN YOU

and i'm sure it kills you that you couldn't keep me

small.

it's okay to love the wrong person
it isn't a waste of time

after all
that is how you learn
what it is that makes
somebody
right
for you

one day back in 2016
i took a match to you and me

i waited for the fire
to catch and spread
waited for flames
to engulf that thread

i waited for the ashes
for the sign that i was free
i waited for years
but couldn't burn away your hold on me

so i left it there
us forever tied
thinking i was doomed
to always have you on my mind

but finally
after many long years
filled with healing and learning
and lots of tears

i looked back at those candles
saw the fire there
lighting up the thread
that for years had sat bare

i watched it burn
watched it and laughed
a smile on my face as
it finally snapped

you see, they aren't your soulmate
this waiting isn't a sign
sometimes a thread takes a while to burn
because what you really need is time

you were once a ghost that haunted my every waking moment. i was ruined by your absence. i felt the loss of you like a physical wound. i might as well have bled for you. perhaps, in some way, i did. but now, you are nothing more than my cautionary tale. i tell our story as a warning. i say, *please don't do what i did.*

i say, *but if you did, here is how you survive it.*

i learned how to breathe deeply
to stave off panic attacks
how to force myself to eat
even though i didn't want to
because i knew it was good for me
i taught myself to look past
the dream of us i'd clung to
and carve a new path that you
wouldn't ever walk with me
i discovered my vagus nerve
conquered sleepless nights
and the swells of anxiety
shaped myself into somebody
you would hardly recognize
forged myself anew in
the fire you set to my life

the key step to healing has always been to grieve. it is easier said than done. grief is a frightening thing, a looming darkness everyone would prefer to avoid. but you must grieve it to accept it and heal from it. if you don't, if you try to hold it back, it will only swell and grow until it crushes the dam you've crafted to restrain it. so you must feel it. yes, the grief will threaten to drown you, for a time. but eventually the tide will recede. your feet will touch the ground again. the shore is not so far away.

they say it takes seven years
for all your skin cells to be replaced
with new ones.

i wonder,

which part of me was the last
to forget your touch?

was it the small of my back
or the underside of my wrist?

the dip of my collarbone
or the tip of my nose?

which part of me
clung to you the longest?

which part of me
was the first to let you go?

to be a poet is to be cursed—
bitten by the worst serpent of all,
poisoned with want,
veins dripping with the
venom of longing, of soul-splitting
desire and self-righteous fury—

do you think i wanted *this*?
do you think i fell at the altar
of creation and begged for
a lifetime spent yearning,
sentenced to ponder each
beginning, each middle
and each end,
destined to sew my
own wounds shut
and then rip them open
again and again
and again—

and it's not my fault i'm a poet,
but it is my fault i've let it ruin my life,
i wrote once, when i should have
been too young to feel this torturous
weight, but love makes Atlases of us all,
each of us condemned titans in our own
self-inflicted, rotten ways.

i would exorcise this from me
if i could. if i could unclench
my fists and let it all go, i swear to you
i would do it in a heartbeat
but do you see, do you understand

that this—all of this haunted memory—
this is the cost of the words?
this is the price i pay for the ink and quill?
but i signed that contract with blood and
i did not read the fine print.

if i'd known when i first set down this path,
perhaps i never would have done it.
if i'd known the way old loves
would cling to me like ticks,
sucking the life out of me
even now, even after years,
perhaps i would have turned away.
grabbed onto monotony with glee,
rejected romanticism and run eagerly
down the path of mundanity
and lived oh-so-happily, unpossessed by the need
to feel *every fucking thing* that has ever happened
to me with such intensity it makes my bones creak,
to never know what it's like to sit and stew
over moments long since passed and lovers
long since left and conversations long since over.
and to be unburdened by the insatiable desperation
to make it all so beautiful—
oh, to be free of that chain. there are days
when i would give anything to break it.

and yet, i do not know how to be anything else.
i am, for better or for worse, a poet. i sometimes
wish the knife of my reality could be dulled,
that the fire inside would burn through me
with less ravenous hunger, but my essence is shaped
around that flame. and what beauty has come from
the ashes it creates.

to be a poet is to be cursed, that much is true.
but to be consumed by the want of love,
by the desire to feel it all—it is not so bad,
in the end.

— *the poet's lament*

it's strange—
the way i remember it now.
it comes to me in pieces.
a kaleidoscope of memory.
never quite the full picture,
not anymore.
but just enough to recall
the feeling.
to catch a flash of color.
a glimpse of the past.

i wish i could go back
and tell my younger self that
her life would become
infinitely more beautiful
the second she loosed
her white-knuckle grip
on the dream she carried
about you

i used to be able to
write about you endlessly.

i could reach into
the part of myself
that loved you—
loved you even then,
even after everything—
and come up with something
kind to say, something wistful.

or i could crack open
the part of myself
that hated you so
intensely i had to lock
it away out of fear
it would consume me.

i could take a journey
into the black crevice
of grief inside me,
or a dive into my
deep sea of confusion.

i once had a never-ending
supply of emotion to
dip my quill into.

now i am empty.

and thank fucking god
for that.

and if you learn one thing
from me and nothing else
let it be that
no wound bleeds
forever

love ends and it is the end of the world.
love ends and it is a gaping wound.
love ends and it is an aching heart.
love ends and it is a never-ending sob.

love ends and it is a prayer.
love ends and it is a deep breath.
love ends and it is a beginning.
love ends and it is a new day.

love ends and it is a question.

love ends and it is an answer.

sometimes i think about what i would say if i were to ever see you again. which, if life isn't cruel, won't happen, but life is cruel, so i'm just counting down the days. i used to think maybe i'd scream at you, but then i did see you and i hardly made a sound. for a while i thought i'd just run in the other direction, but i'm always too nice to people that don't deserve my kindness. there was even a point where the thought of running into you made me feel sick.

it's been about seven years since we were last in the same room together. i've done a lot of healing since then. your name no longer makes my stomach churn. seeing your face doesn't make me see red anymore. you know, there's even been times when you've come up and i've laughed, when you've felt so insignificant i didn't even have to fake a grin. so i think, if i saw you now, i would smile, all saccharine and peachy. i would ask how you've been. and you would say, "good," or "fine," and i would say, "i'm so glad to hear it," and you would ask the same to me, always so polite, and i would look at you with the strength that's born from a million tears, from a hundred scars, and i would say,

"me? well, i'm better than ever."

vii.

and one day
after years of stitching
mending tears
and changing patterns
somebody will come along
and they will settle at your side

when they reach for you
it will not be to take the needle
it will be to place their hands over yours
and say

let's make something beautiful
together

you don't read my poems anymore

after maria giesbrecht

so i must update you:

i am still a professional at leaving people. i've realized there was a lot of good in you i didn't appreciate and a lot of bad i didn't want to recognize. i finally got away from small towns and not-quite cities. i have an apartment with big windows that overlooks the train. i'm comfortable with crowds. i still bite my nails until they bleed. my life is filled with more love than you could have ever given me, no matter how hard you tried, because the people in it actually like me in a way you never did. maybe you've figured that out by now. i have. i'm almost done writing that novel i told you about. i still pace my living room when i'm thinking hard. i'm starting to desire a peaceful life more than a busy one. you were right, what you said about me that one time—i want too much for myself, although i never thought it was a bad thing like you did. i don't have as much trouble sleeping anymore. i work 4 jobs just to pay my rent, but i love each one. i am the happiest i've ever been. i understand why you hated me at the end, but i will still never apologize for leaving. it is what i do best, after all.

love is my friends putting on another marvel movie to keep me from crying over my ex-boyfriend. love is "you'll be fine because that's who you are." love is how she let me go. love is his anger, however warped and furious. love is sometimes not understanding but accepting that you can't change it. love is letting the tears fall. love is admitting that you cared, even when you know you shouldn't have. love is trying. love is honesty. love is offering yourself forgiveness. love is you. love is me. love is all of us.

it's a heavy task, to both bury a love and plant a new one with the same hands. i've got dirt under my nails from a grave and a garden, though it all looks the same under the light. which crumb comes from what once was, which crumb comes from what might be? i find, most days, i cannot be bothered with figuring it out. it is all still grief, is it not? even the hopeful bits. *it is all still grief.*

i think we knew each other in
a past life

i don't have another explanation
for why we reach for each other
the way we do

there's a word—*inyeon.* it's korean. it means "fate." the idea that certain relationships are forged over many lifetimes. it's why you click so well with some people, why you get the feeling that you've known them forever when you've only just met. perhaps it's why you find your paths crossing over and over again, your story never quite finished. it's all part of a story that's been told a million times before in a million different timelines.

it's comforting, isn't it? to know that your time with somebody is never really over. somewhere out there, in another life, you are sitting by their side. the sun is shining, and they are smiling, and everything is as it should be.

the day we met, i spent the whole drive home racking my brain for when i'd met you before. there was something so familiar about you. *i know you,* i'd thought to myself as i'd studied your face. but how?

there was no way our paths had crossed before. and yet, looking at you was like looking into the eyes of my oldest friend.

i was jaded when i met you. the pull i felt didn't do much to change that. it was, as far as i was concerned, a pull i'd felt before, and how had that ended? every story ended the same. every love looked the same when it was nothing but dust.

but i soon realized that this was different. you were different. and that both relieved and terrified me. if you were not like the rest, that meant you were either my salvation or my complete and utter destruction.

it was as if
my soul had stepped
up to a mirror
and standing
in the reflection
staring back

was you

— *other half*

perhaps
you were already
threaded into
my being
before we ever
even met

i had held a love
like this once before.

how i'd grieved
when it had slipped
through my fingers,
how i'd despaired
that i had lost
my chance.

but love comes back.
love *always* comes back.

this time, love came back stronger. it came back prepared. ready for the blows life might deliver. it was not so starry-eyed as before. and for that, i was grateful. i did not want naïveté anymore. i wanted realistic. i wanted stability.

i still wanted romance, of course, but i'd had my fair share of passionate affairs that toppled over the moment the wind blew too strong. i wanted a love with a foundation. i wanted a love that would let me put down roots.

some things that made me realize you were different:

1. when i told you that i needed time, that i needed something slow, you said, "you set the pace and i'll meet you there."
2. when i was sick, you came over and cooked me chicken noodle soup from scratch. we weren't even together yet. you brought me tea to sip on while you cooked. you even did the dishes after.
3. you actually read the book i let you borrow. we talked about it in detail.
4. my apartment was a mess. i was working twelve-hour days. i came home and you'd cleaned the kitchen and changed my sheets. there was fresh flowers and a handwritten note on the counter.
5. the first time i cried in front of you, you didn't flinch away or look anywhere but me.
6. the slow realization that you will never raise your voice nor your hands against me.
7. when we talked about the futures we envisioned for ourselves, it didn't feel like either of us would have to sacrifice a huge part of ourselves to have that future together.
8. in all honesty, there are a dozen tiny moments every single day that remind me of just how special you are, and how lucky i am. if i started keeping track, i could fill a book with them.

when you learn
that love is not
transactional

you learn
just how many
people are
undeserving
of your affection

don't waste time feeling angry towards your past self for not knowing better. they were dancing with love the only way they knew how. so what if they stumbled? so what if they didn't know all the right steps? they were brave enough to take love's hand. they were daring enough to give it a try, even if it wasn't as graceful as they hoped it would be.

you'll know they're the one
not by the sparks that fly between you
or the red hot passion that burns
or the way your heart flutters around them.

it will be the ease that tells you.
it will be the simplicity.
it will be the fact that
you don't even have
to ask for good treatment;
you don't have to beg
for scraps or seconds.

they will give you all
you deserve and more
without you ever
having to say a word.

and that
is how
you will know.

and this time
as i built a home
for somebody
in my heart
it felt solid

like it could withstand
the storms life can bring

like it just might last
forever

i suppose if the multiverse exists there's likely a universe out there where i marry each of the people i've loved. there's a timeline where it worked with each one. and i hope i'm happy in them, though for some, i can't imagine how. perhaps i am unrecognizable. perhaps they are. perhaps it's a bit of both.

but as much as i find comfort in the thought that that could be true, that each version of myself got to be with the person she believed to be her great love, i am so, so glad that i ended up in this one.

little universes

i. august

the neighbor's baby is crying. in the garden next door, the retired professor and his wife host a dinner party. i watch them laugh over their wine under the string lights from my back porch. somebody else is cooking with their door open; the scent of spiced vegetables and smoking meat wafts through the air. distantly, a dog barks. the air is hot even after sunset. life tastes limitless on my tongue.

ii. october

the soft, thoughtful hum of conversation in a bookstore. i run my fingers down spines and tell you which ones i've already read. you ask me about my favorites. i pull richard siken off the shelf. here, the books sing, but so do you. outside, the leaves are orange and red, dappling the streets. it is sunny, the breeze a welcome chill. the train jerks us back and forth on the ride home. i stumble into your side. we laugh, not caring if people are watching.

iii. march

the neighbor's baby is crying. you are cutting open a pomegranate in the kitchen, fingers stained red. the dishwasher is running. a book sits open on my lap. i watch you from the couch. downstairs, somebody is having people over; their laughter floats up through the floorboards. you bring me the seeds when you're finished. i kiss the juice from your fingertips. i taste a million possibilities.

viii.

at the end of your life
you will look back on
the tapestry
you've created

it will be unique
in some parts
it will be messy
bits and pieces
sewn together
into uneven patchwork

but it will be yours

every stitch
every knot
all of it

yours

if you really know yourself
which one would you pick?

i wonder if i would choose
to forget it ever happened
or if i'd choose to understand
why it did

would i decide to forgive them
or simply to have never met them
at all?

would i choose to sit down
with my younger self
(i can't save her)
and hold her and tell her
i'm sorry and i tried my best?

maybe i would pick the option
to stop being the one
who leaves
(but that would mean
i would be getting left)

would i decide to
try again?

would i choose forgiveness?
would i choose acceptance?
would i choose closure?
would i choose understanding?

all these options i have

to erase the little pointed
bits of me

are they not just what
shaped me into who i am?
(is that even a good thing?)

i think i would choose to
see it as a good thing

"everything i've ever let go of has claw marks on it."
after david foster wallace

isn't that the truth.

claw marks and ink stains
and half-written poems and
empty promises and withered apologies
and unanswered questions and
lifelong bitterness and endless grief
and unending wonder and
ageless gratitude and still,
somehow,
amongst all of that—

love.

i don't think
about any of them
the same way
anymore.

the other night
one of them appeared
to me in a dream
and i did not run,
did not fall from sweet sleep
into screaming nightmare.

just kept breathing.
kept dreaming.

when i woke up,
i could feel that they'd been there,
picking through memories,
and i didn't mind.

they come and ago
as they please now,
but they no longer leave
a mess behind.

i hope they all
find their soulmates
and i hope they fall
onto soft downy feathers
the way we once thought
we would

i hope they think of me
as fondly as i dare to
think of them

but if they don't
i hope they forgive me
and i hope they are
as grateful as i am
that they didn't chase me
when i left

unfortunately i am a lover girl

love is my blood
my breath
my voice

love is my reason
to live
to try
to laugh

the love inside me
is what makes me beautiful
it's what makes me kind
and soft and understanding
and i have always wanted
to share it with others

so yes
i love love
i love being in love
i love falling in love

part of me even loves
picking myself up off the ground
when it's over because that means
i get to experience it all again

and i wouldn't give up
this part of my soul
for anything

-lover girl

because
if it's not all for love
then what the fuck
is it for?

so maybe being a lover girl
isn't such an unfortunate thing
after all?

maybe the answer to everything
has always just been love

and the lover girls are the ones
fortunate enough to know it
from the very second they are born?

when i take a moment to think about all the people i've loved, i also think about all the people i have been. at times i was so different i hardly recognize myself when i look at the snapshots of memories. but other times, often with people i no longer speak to, there's a glimpse. a fraction of a second, but i see it all the same.

A VENN DIAGRAM

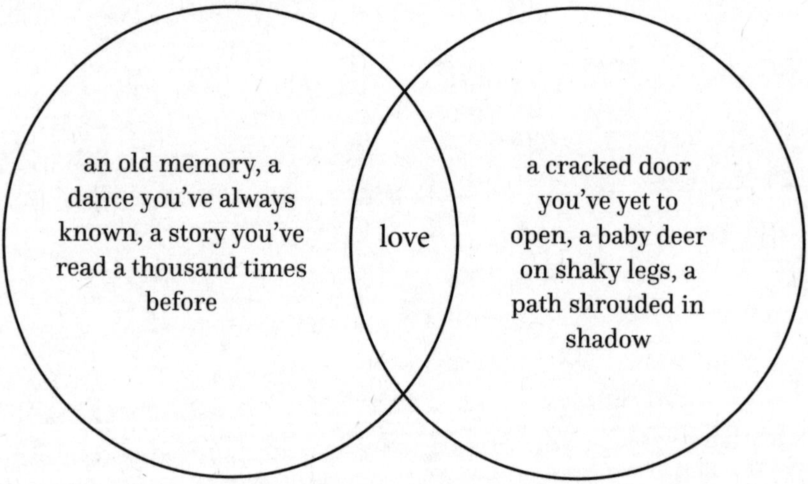

so thank you to all of them
both the bad and the good
thank you to the liars
the cheats and the cruel
thank you to the lovers
the loyal and the kind
thank you for showing me
the dos and the don'ts
thank you for helping me realize
what love is and what love isn't
no matter which side of the line you fall
thank you for whatever you gave me
and you can keep whatever it is
that you took in return

do you see it now?
do you understand that
the answer has always been

love?

and though you hurt,
life continues on.

time heals all wounds
eventually.

and one day,
you'll look around
and think,

it's so good!

it's so good.

Catarine Hancock, a poet, author, and opera singer from Lexington, Kentucky, now living in Chicago, began writing poetry at thirteen and has since built a significant online platform alongside her five poetry collections and a fantasy romance novel. When she's not singing or writing, you can find her curled up with a fantasy novel, browsing local bookstores, or adding quirky Goodwill finds to her already too-cluttered apartment.

Find her at @catarinehancock

Thank you to my family and friends for buying my books, telling everyone they know about them, and shouting from the rooftops about how proud they are of me. There were times when that was the only thing pushing me through a creative slump.

Thank you to Matt, my lovely partner, for giving me a reason to write love poems again, and for always being ready to listen to whatever new idea I'd come up with.

Thank you to Michelle and the team at Central Avenue for always being so supportive and believing in my poetry. I'll be honest, I hear a lot of horror stories about publishing, and I feel very lucky that I can't relate to a single one of them. Thank you to my fellow poets for beta reading and blurbing my collections, including this one, and for being such a lovely, uplifting community. I'm so thankful I have peers I can come to for support, advice, and at times, commiseration. It's been so wonderful watching all of our careers blossom over the last several years.

And last but not least, thank you to my readers. You are the reason I get to live my dream of being a published author. Thank you for every follow, like, comment, and share, every picture of one of my books, every kind DM, every time you recommend one of my books to somebody. I would not be where I am without you. It's been twelve years of us—can you believe that? Here's to many, many more.

also by catarine hancock

shades of lovers
sometimes i fall asleep thinking about you
sprout
i gave myself the world
holy ground

curse of stolen flame: a novel